William Kidd

and the
Pirates of the Indian Ocean

John Malam

QEB Publishing

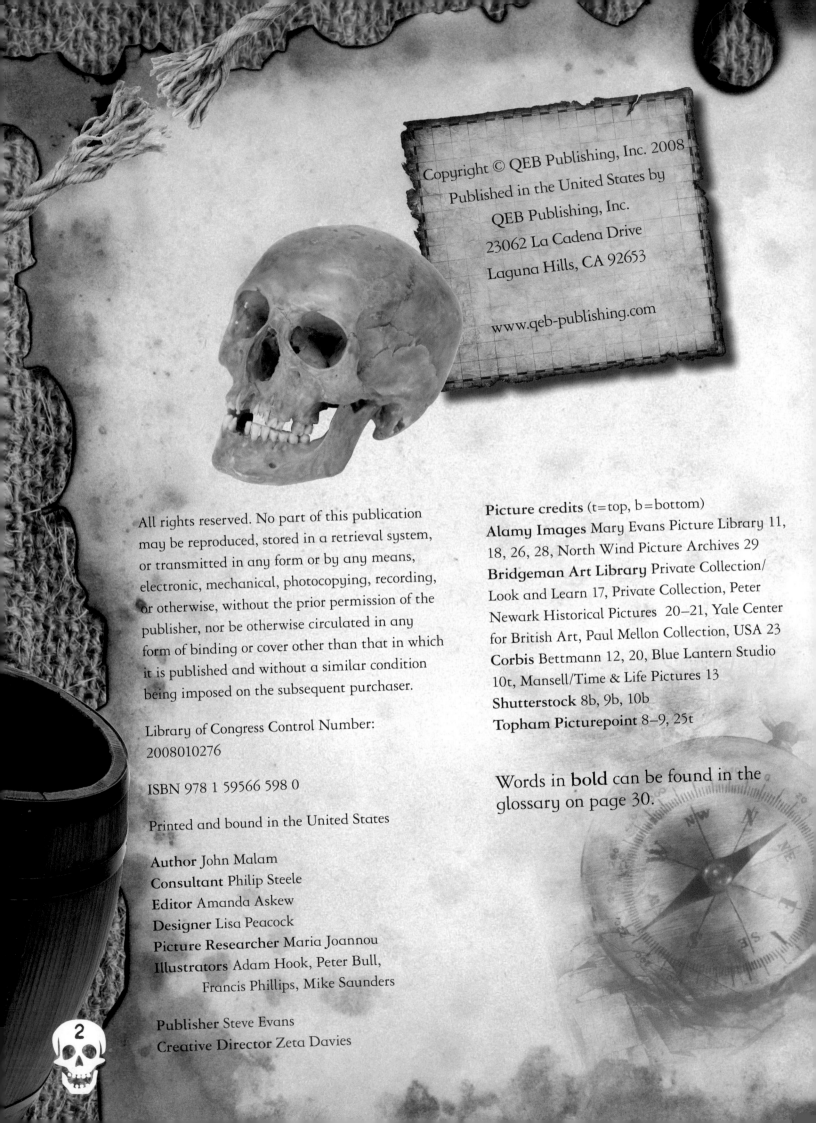

Library of Congress Control Number: 2008010276

ISBN 978 1 59566 598 0

Printed and bound in the United States

Author John Malam
Consultant Philip Steele
Editor Amanda Askew
Designer Lisa Peacock
Picture Researcher Maria Joannou
Illustrators Adam Hook, Peter Bull,
        Francis Phillips, Mike Saunders

Publisher Steve Evans
Creative Director Zeta Davies

Picture credits (t=top, b=bottom)
Alamy Images Mary Evans Picture Library 11, 18, 26, 28, North Wind Picture Archives 29
Bridgeman Art Library Private Collection/ Look and Learn 17, Private Collection, Peter Newark Historical Pictures 20–21, Yale Center for British Art, Paul Mellon Collection, USA 23
Corbis Bettmann 12, 20, Blue Lantern Studio 10t, Mansell/Time & Life Pictures 13
Shutterstock 8b, 9b, 10b
Topham Picturepoint 8–9, 25t

Words in **bold** can be found in the glossary on page 30.

Contents

Pirate attack!

William Kidd was supposed to be hunting pirates in the Indian Ocean, but he became a pirate himself.

As he turned the *Adventure Galley* toward the large **merchant ship** sailing near the west coast of India, he was about to seize the greatest **prize** of his pirating career.

It was January 1698, and the *Adventure Galley*, despite her rotten and leaky hull, was soon upon the *Quedah Merchant*. As she closed in, Kidd raised French flags. It was an old trick, which the captain of the *Quedah Merchant* fell for —the false flags made him think that Kidd's ship was friendly. Kidd went aboard the *Quedah Merchant* without a struggle, and told its captain that he was claiming the ship as his prize. In the ship's hold was a valuable **cargo** of silk, **calico**, sugar, iron, guns, and gold coins.

◀ *William Kidd's* Adventure Galley *closes in on the* Quedah Merchant, *an Indian trading ship. Kidd sold most of the cargo for $13,000 and kept the captured ship for himself.*

After selling most of the cargo at a port in India, Kidd sailed the *Quedah Merchant* to the pirate **haven** of Madagascar, where he fitted it out with **cannon** from the *Adventure Galley*. He renamed the ship the *Adventure Prize* and it became his new **flagship**.

5

Pirates of the Indian Ocean: 1690–1720

India

Arabia

AFRICA

Indian Ocean

Madagascar

Réunion

For about 30 years, from 1690 to 1720, the Indian Ocean was a pirates' paradise.

Some of the pirates were local people, such as Conajee Angria who was based on the west coast of India. Other pirates came from Europe, including William Kidd, Edward England, Henry Every, and Thomas Tew. Some, such as Edward England, had begun their piracy in the Caribbean before moving east to try their luck in new waters. The European pirates used the islands of Madagascar and Réunion, off the east coast of Africa, as their havens. It was safe to moor their ships and go ashore there.

◄ *In the early years of the 18th century, countless ships were plundered by pirates as they crossed the Indian Ocean.*

▲ *A pirate's favourite weapon for hand-to-hand fighting was the cutlass. It was a sword with a short, broad blade.*

ROGUES' GALLERY

Henry Every
Active as a pirate
1692–1695

Thomas Tew
Active as a pirate
1692–1695

Edward England
Active as a pirate
1717–1720

SHIVER ME TIMBERS!

Pirates of the Indian Ocean were probably the most successful pirates in history. When it came to sharing out the **loot**, each man probably received about $2,000. Pirates in the Caribbean were lucky to get $40!

William Kidd
Active as a pirate
1697–1699

Pirates sailed in the Indian Ocean because it offered them the chance to get rich—many merchant ships crossed the ocean to take valuable goods to the markets of Europe. The scoundrels also robbed **vessels** taking Muslim **pilgrims** to Arabia, and ships carrying cargoes to India.

In search of prey

There was one type of ship that Indian Ocean pirates preyed on more than any other.

It was a merchant ship called an **East Indiaman**. Pirates regarded these large, slow-moving vessels as their prizes. East Indiamen were cargo ships sent by countries in Europe to collect valuable goods from countries in Asia. As they sailed east toward Asia across the Indian Ocean, pirates searched for them. They knew that on board would be silver coins, and possibly gold **ingots**, which were to be traded for goods. A single ship might be carrying as much as $100,000 (about $10 million in today's money) in silver and gold.

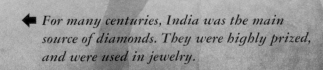

← *For many centuries, India was the main source of diamonds. They were highly prized, and were used in jewelry.*

The East Indiamen were most vulnerable on their way home. Heavy with cargo, they were slow-moving targets for plundering pirates. To protect themselves, these ships were armed with cannon. They often sailed in **convoys**, or groups, and sometimes they were guarded by navy warships.

SHIVER ME TIMBERS!

In 1721, English pirate John Taylor captured the *Nostra Senhora de Cabo* at the island of Réunion. The Portuguese ship was carrying goods worth $1.7 million. It was the biggest haul ever taken by a pirate in the Indian Ocean.

◄ *East Indiamen were large, heavy ships that sat low in the water. Smaller, lighter ships were used to carry cargoes to and from them.*

▲ *Cannonballs were fired by East Indiamen. They were made from solid iron and smashed through the hull and masts of enemy ships.*

Treasures of the east

There were rich pickings for pirates who sailed in the Indian Ocean.

East Indiamen ships sailing back to Europe were loaded with cargoes of spice, tea, silk, ivory, diamonds, rubies, and **porcelain**. All of these were luxury goods that only the richest people in Europe could afford to buy. Some of this **booty** could be very bulky, so pirates didn't want to hold onto it for very long. They usually sold it in local markets—as William Kidd did when he sold most of the cargo from the *Quedah Merchant* in an Indian market for about $14,000.

⬇ *According to legend, William Kidd buried a haul of treasure somewhere in the Indian Ocean. Treasure hunters have searched for it, without success.*

◀ *Spices and tea took up a lot of room on a ship and could be difficult for pirates to sell. They often dumped these goods into the sea.*

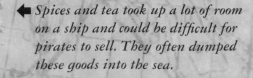

*An East Indiaman cargo ship
sinks to the bottom of the sea after
being raided by pirates in the
Indian Ocean.*

It didn't take
pirates of the
Indian Ocean long
to discover what
treasures were carried
on board **pilgrim ships**. Each
year, a fleet of 20 or 30 ships sailed
from India to Arabia, taking Muslims on the first stage of their
journey to the holy city of Mecca. Indian merchants traveled
with the pilgrims to Arabia, where they traded cloth and spice
for gold and jewels. On their way back to India, the pilgrim
ships became easy targets for European pirates.

SHIVER ME TIMBERS!

In 1695, Henry Every raided the Indian treasure ship *Gang-i-Sawai* in the Red Sea. He got away with gold and jewels said to be worth $650,000— billions in today's money.

William Kidd: the unlucky pirate

William Kidd never set out to be a pirate. For many years, he worked as a privateer in the Caribbean, where he had permission to raid French ships.

He did a good job and became quite well known. In 1695, he traveled to London and went into business with two men. They gave him a ship, the *Adventure Galley*. The plan was for Kidd to catch pirates, take their loot, then share it with his business partners. The plan didn't work.

← *Kidd fought with William Moore, hitting him with a bucket bound with iron hoops.*

Soon after the *Adventure Galley* entered the Indian Ocean, Kidd's **crew** tried to take control. Kidd hit one of the **mutineers**, William Moore, with a wooden bucket and killed him. Kidd continued on his journey, but instead of catching pirates he seized the *Quedah Merchant*.

Kidd thought he would be safe in the United States, but he wasn't. He was sent to England to stand trial for his crimes.

It was an Indian merchant ship, and by attacking without permission, Kidd had become a pirate. He kept the *Quedah Merchant* and gave her a new name—the *Adventure Prize*. Kidd sailed the *Adventure Prize* to America, where he was arrested and sent to London, England, to be tried as a pirate and a murderer. He was found guilty and sentenced to death.

William Kidd

Born: c.1645, in Scotland

Died: 1701, in London

Occupation: Privateer and pirate

13

The Adventure Galley: a pirate rowing ship

In 1695, William Kidd took command of the Adventure Galley, a three-masted vessel with a crew of about 150 men.

It was designed for sailing fast, but when the wind didn't fill the sails, there was another way to move the wooden ship through the water. The ship was a **galley**, which meant it had oars. On calm days, the crew pulled on 36 oars and rowed it along. It was hard, back-breaking work, but it meant the *Adventure Galley* could close in on ships when there was no wind. Enemy ships would be going nowhere, but all the time the *Adventure Galley* would be rowing closer to them.

Ship's lantern

Mizzen mast

Gunport

➡ *Cross-section through Kidd's first ship, the* Adventure Galley, *showing its decks, guns, and oars.*

Powder and shot store

SHIVER ME TIMBERS!

In 1999, a shipwreck was discovered in a bay on Madagascar. The ship had been burned, so it could be the wreck of the *Adventure Galley*.

Unfortunately for Kidd, the *Adventure Galley* was a leaky ship. He sailed it to Madagascar where he removed all the cannon, set it on fire, and left it to sink. He put the cannon on his new ship, the *Adventure Prize*.

Foremast

Bowsprit

Main mast

Rowers

Adventure Galley

Built: 1695, Deptford shipyard, London

Abandoned: 1698, Madagascar

Weight: 285 tons

Length: 125 feet

Masts: 3

Guns: 34 cannon

Drinking water casks

Oars

15

A hard life at sea

When a man agreed to become a sea-robber, he signed the ship's articles, which was a list of rules.

The pirates who sailed with William Kidd signed articles that promised them a share of any booty taken from a prize ship. However, if they didn't obey orders, they would be punished according to the rules —**marooning** was to be left on a remote island and **keel-hauling** was to be dragged under the ship.

SHIVER ME TIMBERS!

A pirate captain dreaded the rumbling sound of a cannonball rolling across the ship's deck. It was a signal from the crew that they were going to take control— a **mutiny** was about to happen.

← If a man didn't drown while being keel-hauled, he might die later from cuts caused as he was dragged across sharp barnacles on the ship's hull.

↑ *The crew on a pirate ship worked hard, under the captain's orders.*

A pirate ship could be away at sea for many months. This was always tough on the crew, as food and water would start to run out and they would have to go onto **rations**. There might be problems with the ship, as with Kidd's *Adventure Galley*, which was scrapped because of its rotten hull. Worst of all, the pirates might not find a prize, which could lead to unrest.

Articles of William Kidd

1. If a man loses an eye, leg, or arm, he shall receive 600 pieces of eight, or six able slaves.
2. The man who is first to see the sail of a prize ship shall receive 100 pieces of eight.
3. Any man who disobeys a command shall lose his share and be punished as the captain deems fit.
4. Any man proved a coward in time of engagement shall lose his share.
5. Any man drunk in time of engagement shall lose his share.
6. Any man that talks of mutiny shall lose his share and be punished as the captain deems fit.
7. Any man that cheats the captain or company of any treasure, money, goods, or any other thing whatsoever to the value of one piece of eight shall lose his share and be left upon the first inhabited island the ship shall touch at.
8. Any money or treasure taken shall be shared amongst the ship's company.

Thomas Tew: the Rhode Island pirate

Thomas Tew was one of the pirates that William Kidd was supposed to catch, but never did.

Tew was based at Rhode Island, and like Kidd, he started as a **privateer** before turning to piracy. Tew's ship, the *Amity*, was a **sloop**. This was a small, fast vessel that was perfect for pirates.

Thomas Tew

Born: date not known, in England

Died: 1695, in the Red Sea

Occupation: Privateer and pirate

In 1694, Thomas Tew (left) visited Benjamin Fletcher (right), the governor of New York. Tew presented Fletcher with jewels that he had plundered from ships in the Red Sea.

In 1693, Tew captured a valuable Indian merchant ship in the Red Sea. He plundered its gold and gemstones, and threw the rest of the bulky cargo overboard as it was of no value to him. The haul of treasure was shared between the ship's **company**, and each man received $6,000— a huge amount of money for the time.

⬆ *The pirate flag of Thomas Tew.*

⬅ *Tew met a grizzly end. He was blown apart by a cannonball fired from the* Fateh Mohammed *as he tried to take over the ship.*

Tew joined up with Henry Every, another pirate of the Indian Ocean. They put together a small fleet of pirate ships and began to plague the Red Sea —but not for long. In 1695, during an attack on an Indian vessel, Tew was killed by a cannonball that hit him in the stomach.

Henry Every: the successful pirate

Very few pirates got away with their crimes, except for Henry Every.

He was a master of disguise who used a false name—his real name might have been Benjamin Bridgeman, which is why one of his nicknames was "Long Ben."

⬆ *Henry Every's success as a pirate in the Indian Ocean earned him a fortune. In the background, his ship attacks a treasure ship.*

Every began as a privateer in the Caribbean, raiding French settlements on the island of Martinique. All this changed in 1694, when he led a mutiny and took control of a ship, which he renamed the *Fancy*. He then sailed into the Indian Ocean, where he teamed up with Thomas Tew and other European pirates.

His greatest prize was the *Gang-i-Sawai*, an Indian treasure ship in the Red Sea. After a battle lasting two hours, the merchant ship surrendered, and Every helped himself to $1.2 million in gold, silver, and gems. After the booty was shared among the pirate fleet, Every sailed back to the Caribbean and disappeared.

▼ *Every led a fleet of pirate ships. They preyed on Muslim pilgrim ships returning to India with luxury goods, gold, and silver.*

SHIVER ME TIMBERS!

Some of Every's crew returned to England, where they were caught and hanged. As for Every, it is thought that he settled in Ireland, where he changed his identity and lived off his ill-gotten gains.

Henry Every, known as "Long Ben"

Born: c.1653, in England

Died: date and place not known

Occupation: Pirate

Madagascar: a pirate haven

William Kidd knew he would be safe once he reached Madagascar.

This large island, off the east coast of Africa, was a haven for pirates, and it was where Kidd abandoned the leaky *Adventure Galley* in 1698. Madagascar was on a busy **trade route**, and East Indiamen sailing to and from Europe and North America sailed close by. Each passing merchant ship was a potential prize for a plundering pirate.

Pirate colonies grew up on the east side of Madagascar, and by 1720 there were about 1,500 pirates there. Many had fled to Madagascar from the Caribbean, after the authorities there had clamped down on them. Traders worked in the colonies, selling everyday goods to pirates in exchange for their stolen booty.

⬆ *On Madagascar, European traders sold guns, swords, gunpowder, and alcohol to the island's pirates.*

↑ *Squadrons of British battleships were sent to Madagascar—the pirates were no match for these heavily-armed ships with men trained for war.*

The pirates became such a nuisance that something had to be done to protect shipping. In the 1720s, warships of the British Royal Navy began cruising near Madagascar, and the pirate menace faded away.

SHIVER ME TIMBERS!

Life was hard for pirates on Madagascar. They were often killed by disease, or in fights with local people or pirate gangs.

The Angrias: a family of pirates

Pirates from Europe were not the only menace in the Indian Ocean—there were also plenty of local pirates.

The most notorious was the Angria family, who plundered ships of all nations. Piracy was their way of life, passed on from father to son. The Angrias were masters of the west coast of India for about 50 years, from 1700 to 1750. They stopped ships that crossed into their territory and forced the captains to give them money. In return, the Angrias let the ships carry on their journeys —but not always.

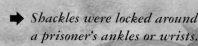

➡ *Shackles were locked around a prisoner's ankles or wrists.*

SHIVER ME TIMBERS!

Conajee Angria kept an English merchant, Peter Curgenven, captive for about five years. He had to wear chains called **shackles**, which injured his legs. When Curgenven was released, a doctor cut off his worst leg and Curgenven bled to death.

In 1704, the British told Conajee Angria to leave their ships alone. He refused. In 1707, he attacked the *Bombay*, a British East Indiaman, and he went on to raid many others. In 1736, Conajee's son, Sumbhajee, plundered the *Derby* and a fortune in gold was seized. The end came in 1756, when a fleet of British warships destroyed 65 Angria pirate ships and took their treasure.

⬆ *The Angria fleet (the smaller ships) attacked British merchant ships off the coast of India in 1740.*

Conajee Angria

Born: date not known, in India

Died: 1729, in India

Occupation: Pirate

⬅ *Conajee Angria was the leader of a family of Indian pirates.*

Edward England:
the kind-hearted pirate

Edward England became a pirate in 1717, when pirates took over the ship he was on —he decided to join them.

At first, England worked as a pirate in the Caribbean, until he was forced to flee in 1718. He sailed to Africa, where he plundered ships along the west coast and in the Indian Ocean.

➡ *In one raid, England used a fireship (a burning ship) against two vessels he hoped to capture. The plan failed, and the ships escaped.*

England gave one of his prize ships to one of his crew, John Taylor. In 1720, England attacked the *Cassandra*, a British East Indiaman. In the battle, off the coast of Madagascar, 90 of England's pirate crew were killed, but they managed to seize the *Cassandra*.

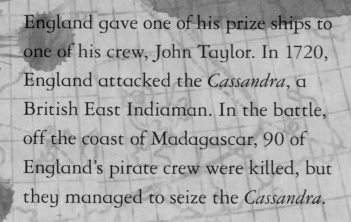

Edward England

Born: date not known, in Ireland

Died: c.1721, on Madagascar

Occupation: Pirate

England took the cargo, said to be worth $150,000. He let the crew go free, which made John Taylor very angry. He said that England should have killed the crew in revenge for the loss of so many of their pirate comrades. The men agreed with Taylor, and they made him their captain, in place of England.

➡ *The pirate flag of Edward England.*

Most pirates came to miserable ends.

Thomas Tew was killed by a cannonball, Edward England spent his last days as a beggar, and William Kidd was hanged—not once, but twice. If a pirate was caught by the authorities, he was almost certain to be sentenced to death, and that meant being hanged by the neck until dead.

⬇ The trial of William Kidd was held in London, England, in 1701.

In 1699, William Kidd was arrested in Boston, and was sent to trial in England. At this time, parts of North America were controlled by England, which is why his trial was held there. In May 1701, Kidd was found guilty of murdering William Moore, the sailor he hit with a bucket, and of robbing the *Quedah Merchant*.

Kidd was sentenced to hang. On the first attempt, the hangman's rope snapped, and Kidd fell to the ground, very much alive. He was led back up to the **scaffold**, and a new noose was put around his neck. This one didn't break.

↓ *Kidd's dead body was hanged in chains—an iron cage that kept his remains together while they slowly rotted away.*

SHIVER ME TIMBERS!

Kidd's body was placed inside an iron cage and left to hang on the shore of the Thames River at Tilbury, near London, England. Birds pecked at the body and it slowly rotted. It was a grizzly sight, meant to stop other men from becoming pirates.

GLOSSARY

Articles
A set of rules that pirates were expected to follow.

Booty
Goods stolen by thieves. Another word for loot or plunder.

Calico
A type of fine cotton fabric.

Cannon
A large gun on wheels that fired cannonballs and other types of shot.

Cargo
The goods carried on a ship.

Company
The crew of a pirate ship.

Convoy
A group of ships traveling together.

Crew
The people who worked on a ship. Also called the company.

Cutlass
A short sword with a slightly curved blade.

East Indiaman
A large, slow-moving sailing ship used to transport goods. A merchant ship.

Flagship
The main ship used by a pirate captain or navy commander.

Galley
A type of ship powered through the water by oars.

Haven
A safe place, or a hideaway.

Ingot
A block of metal, such as gold or silver.

Keel-haul
To be hauled or dragged under a ship from one side to the other.

Loot
Goods stolen by thieves. Another word for booty or plunder.

Maroon
To abandon, or leave, on an island.

Merchant ship
A ship designed to transport goods.

Moor

To secure a ship to the shore by means of a rope or cable.

Mutineer

A person who refuses to take orders from a ship's captain.

Mutiny

When the crew take control of a ship from its captain.

Pilgrim

A person making a journey to a holy place.

Pilgrim ship

A ship taking pilgrims to a holy place.

Plunder

To steal, or goods stolen by thieves. Also called loot or booty.

Porcelain

A type of fine, white pottery originally made in China.

Privateer

A person who has permission from his government or ruler to attack and steal goods from his country's enemy.

Prize

A ship taken as a reward.

Rations

A fixed amount of food, usually served each day.

Scaffold

A raised structure that was used to hang criminals them.

Shackles

A pair of metal rings joined by a chain that are used to hold together a prisoner's hands or feet.

Sloop

A small, fast vessel.

Trade route

A way across sea or land that was used by traders.

Vessel

A ship or large boat.

INDEX